I0753536

FINISHING LINE PRESS
www.finishinglinepress.com

De Novo: Starting from the beginning; anew

poems by

Kelly Anne

Finishing Line Press
Georgetown, Kentucky

De Novo: Starting from the beginning; anew

ISBN 979-8-89990-513-1 First Edition

ACKNOWLEDGMENTS

Mine—*Moon Shadow Sanctuary Press*
Thread—*HerStry*
Wish—*Door is A Jar Magazine*
Sleigh Bells; Hot Gun—*Paloma Magazine*
P.E;.The Euphemism—*HNDL Magazine*
Birdling; Unrest—*Vita & the Woolf*

Thank you to my husband, friends and family whose love and support bestows the courage necessary to share my writing.

For Luna—my greatest teacher; may you continue to be exactly who you are and shine brightly in your worthiness. The lessons you continue to teach me and those around you are vast and utterly invaluable.

For Ruby—what a fiercely brave, funny and sensitive soul you are. I am blessed to be your mother and cherish our talks. Your light has filled cracks in my heart and I am forever grateful.

Publisher: Leah Huete de Maines
Editor: Christen Kincaid
Cover Art: Savannah Chase
Author Photo: SG{ Photography
Cover Design: Elizabeth Maines McCleavy

Order online: www.finishinglinepress.com
also available on amazon.com

Author inquiries and mail orders:
Finishing Line Press
PO Box 1626
Georgetown, Kentucky 40324
USA

Contents

In loving memory:

For Nanny—my rock, my everything—this book is dedicated to you. Thank you for your unwavering support and devotion to my wellbeing. I miss and love you immensely.

For Diana—"Beloved" is for you. I will always remember your deep emerald green eyes and precious laugh. You will never be forgotten and continue to inspire all who love you.

Section I: Love & coming of age

The semantics of *fine*

*

To whom am I indebted?
A library book overdue
Tortoise shell frames don a motorcycle cop
A hard helmet like barnacles embedded beneath shoulder blades
When will we be square?

Wispy and frail
A vintage doily with yellowing edges
Water colored flowers born from coffee filters
The under eyes like repurposed tissue paper
A crestfallen eyelash adorning the morning paper

Mediocre at best
Secondhand shoes
Life a pair of socks
Cold blueberry flapjacks
Tuesday

Sparkling wine
Suit and tie
Billowing ball gowns
French cigarettes
Stepping gingerly out of the cab

A lit match
A tall glass of water
Glimmering doe eyes
An unequivocal stare
A mutual sting
*
All of this to exemplify
the architecture of you
So, forget the single teacup
I'll take the entire collection of your variance
And guard it like a prized display
of my best china

Sweet girl

Oh, gin drinker
Your Christmas breath
Hangs heavy on my neck
A cushy scent I swoon
Faint and flimsy
Like a strand of tinsel
Adorning sprigs of pine
Entangled in the letters
That slide off your tongue
I catch them
One-by-one
Spelling your name
Indelibly inscribed
On my soul's heel

Now tell me true
Do you love me
Like I love you?
I'd rather be faceless
Than unlearn the lines in your hands
A bottle of commotion
Warms my bones
Oh, snake charmer
Another round
I'll drink your potion
Or is it poison?
I drop dead
Smitten
Like a sweet girl

Mine

I keep this thought
inside a matchbox
a slow burn
remembers you
a birthday song
stings my eyes
a subtle shrine
I call it mine

A whiskey sip
this dank place
graceless feet
steadily sway
a secret kiss
in a tin locket
the keeper's cry
I call it mine

A timeless rose
pressed and dried
among musk pages
a story refined
oh, rising tide
bathe me holy
a love divine
I call it mine

A simple song
a faithful hymn
night rhythm
keeps lovers awake
but mornings nigh
a mere past life
To treasure
I call it mine

Molasses

The hands of time
Drip like molasses
Slow and steady
Sweet on my tongue
When I'm with you
I am enthralled by the tales you tell
Wondering if someday
You will remember me
With a likened passion
Your eyes are hypnotizing
Like the ring of my grandfather
China blue
A cat eye stone
Your charm is metallic and shiny
Luring me in like a barracuda in the dull sea
From afar I meet your gaze
We move with words around the room
An effortless flow of thought
Twirls me around like a weightless girl
Overhead and inside out
We twist wildly like a tambourine
You pretend you're Fred Astaire
And call me "Ginger baby"
If only we could dance
The way we talk
We'd never leave this place

Electricity

The heels of my feet are possessed
By a free spirit who bears your name
Burning holes in the rug
With the soles of our shoes
We set the room ablaze
Supple limbs like gelatin
Adhere to the shape of you
Sticky with dew
We concurrently groove
Grasping chemistry with bare hands
In this moment
We are reduced to electricity
A fantastical life force
I am awakened
Every time we dance

Thread

We gaze at the moon together
A magical reverie
Asking ourselves what it means
To be here
Together alone
Breathing in tandem
I collect your thoughts like precious stones
For safekeeping
Remnants of your frosty breath hang in the night air
Your voice soothes me asleep
The gentle hum of a violin
Rocks me back and forth
Like a sailboat at sea
A soft ebb and flow
We lay belly up on the bow
Your hand in mine
Like a nostalgic melody
I've known all my life
It feels so natural
Worn and tepid
Like broken leather
You smell of old books with curled up pages
Comforting and familiar
Exuding cool wisdom and playful anecdotes
That transcend your youth
Thirty-two
Refined with age
Questioning father time
Seeking the thread to tie up loose ends
Like catching butterflies in a meadow
Desperate for a glimpse of beauty
I will hold the net
As you let it all go
Open-hearted
Open arms
Nestled inside yourself
Serenity guides you home

Shoreline

We glide atop easy water
Gritting wind between our teeth
Our shoulders burn rosy
Sprouting islands of fresh freckles
Emerald seaweed sits pretty in the belly of the tide
Sea life buzzes like a sunken city
Illuminating the ocean floor
Hermit crabs debut modern shells
Posey pelicans stare
A drunken jelly shimmies slow
I gulp bubbles fast
Cold fizz dances beneath my nose
A hoppy sip of heaven
My fishing rod stands tall
I listen as the line slices the breeze
Whistling like a distant train
I think aloud and ask the sky:
"If paper words could survive nature's fury
would you read them?"
You respond with a glance
& knowing eyes like aged glass
setting on the shoreline

Wish

When I was a girl
I beheld a falling star
Cascading across wine skies
I watched it plunge into woodlands nestled near my home
I hopped on my bike and peddled feverishly
Reaching the forest by dusk
I spent night's hours searching for the starlet
My kid fingers digging tirelessly into earth's mouth
I sang the cricket's songs
Whilst mosquitos drank my blood
At last I found the concrete star
Solidified upon its descent from the atmosphere
I counted all five points
Before smashing it to bits
Heaving the celestial nova against onyx pavement
The rock burst open
Donning jagged edges of shimmering crystals abound
Casting flecks of moonlight in my hair like a kitschy disco ball
"I am a heavenly goddess!"
I placed the fragments in my satchel and carried them to you
Now you can make a wish wherever you choose
Even as a girl,
I wanted you to have all that you desired
I still do

I kept an opalescent slice
affixed to a strand of beaten gold
I do not wish for anything
A token of your bliss is enough

Crushed rose

I'm up late again
Thinking of the velvet rose left wilted on the floor
I bought it for you
To bestow like a wrapped gift
To make you feel treasured
But alas it sat where I left it
In the backseat
Hidden from view
You see, I'm embarrassed of the solitary rose—a soft blush hue
It unveils me until I'm nude in truth
Only an unabashed fool would make such a gesture so bold
Who do I think I am?
I hum dumb to a songbird's tune
Baffled and energized
Buzzing in your brilliance
I drove home alone that night
Dark and winding roads
The DJs were my friends
I left the rose on the lobby floor
It was gone by morning

Oil Slick

Into mystical iris orbs, I stare
Captivated by a winding mosaic path of royal blues & emerald greens
Swirling together like a brilliant oil slick
Its lucid dreams of French Polynesia
Our laughter coated in clover honey
Sugar-sand clinging to your knees
Memories are conjured against my will
The recipient of an unwanted postcard I cannot bear to discard
Documenting the exotic places you've inhabited without me—
I am tethered
Its a calculated gesture cloaked in positive regard
Its wielding power over the powerless
Its motion sickness until my footing is found

Rainbows

Her body bends the light
Casting rainbows upon my skin
I marvel in her beauty
Basking in the colors of our love
I liken her to a mood ring
An indigo ocean of blue
Holding fast until it fades
Vibrantly amber
Flashes of emerald green
Brazen as oozing magma
Hot to the touch
Hardening over time
She can't stay red for long
The cool stone cracks open
Illuminating the glistening pulse
Of her ruby heart
I adore every shade of her
Studying each hue like a devoted pupil
Fascinated by her depth
Frustrated by her shallowness
She carelessly sheds light
Upon a girl I never knew
With the certainty of archery
She's mad about you

Pursuit of Song

I was in pursuit of song but the key was minor and notes fell flat
I can harmonize to make any melody sound pretty
        or palatable
I'bent reality to illuminate a musical fantasy
A Broadway full of phony lines & narratives & characters that appear enticingly true
Do re mi fa-lling-so languidly
Pictured on the outskirts of their mind
Floating faintly in the periphery
A formless fleck
Indiscernible afterthoughts
    all the while they were
                    all I could see
Don McLean told me music dies
A song inevitably ends
though one can listen repeatedly
imprinting lyrics and inflections on the brainstem
a chord change is a timestamp exhuming cached memories
The scent of lemon peel and molasses from grandad's kitchen. 1995. A jagged little pill.
~
I was in the grocery when I heard a bemoaned medley of brass & baritone & Pet Sounds
minding my business in dairy before the tune pierced all five senses just so.
I spotted a gelatin fruit cake—bemused by its function
A bouncy blush mold speckled green
It's pretty like the song
and pointless

Section II: Grief & Loss

Lydia

When Lydia died
I asked for the ocean floor of her purse.
The deepest worn layer littered with bits of sand &

I. A pair of baby socks
II. Two crinkled Dum Dums wrappers
(raspberry and mystery???)

Lydia, solve the mystery
Was it underwhelming (butterscotch) or
as classically pleasing as sour apple?
Were you pirouetting in a hurry?

III. Seven patina incrusted pennies
IV. Four elastic ties with honey hair coiled around the bands like tinsel mingled in Christmas pine

The trappings of her purse tell stories
Trivial relics of her day
showcasing the barrage of errands, she ran
& ran
A guessing game I can play
Coz now there's nothing new and
Lydia, this junk lives and breathes you
So, I'll keep it with mine
& pretend our talks
Aren't just me talking

Beloved

A red thumbtack punctures cork
Fastening her photo in place
With cement conviction
Her eyes of hazel like a lazy lagoon
Are fixed on mine
From every angle of the room
Adjusting my perspective
Like the lens of a camera
Widening the periphery
Inviting the haze to crystallize
Shifting my focus from a stony narrow gorge
To the breadth of the Amazon river
Her image speaks music
The melody of her voice
Resounds in my mind

I reckon I have a choice
To narrate my story
To write this chapter anew
To devour this life
With the zest of a key lime
I dive into tar coffee
Buzzing on the liberty
To caress my beloved
To feel the soft of my baby's cheek
Upon my breast
To rub lotion on her belly
I inhale the sweet aroma
Of wild flowers growing from my legs
Plucking each bloom
A bouquet of life's pleasantries
I am alive

Her being is no longer
But her picture breathes my lungs
She is a sunbeam
Inside of me
Inside of you

Sleigh Bells

"How are you feeling?" the shrink asked.

I compare my insides to a muted trumpet

"Have you ever listened to *Closing Time*...1973?"

That's how.

Doc gazes at me obtusely

—

The vertigo comes on gradually like the brain tolerating pink
powdery pills

Sometimes I listen to the French horn play again & again until I
am lucid and mouthing the words

It's not lost on me that I haven't missed anyone like this since 2014

The year that shattered time's watch

—

"You can hear sleigh bells in *God Only Knows*" she said earnestly.
"That song makes my eyes sting."

~~Precisely, I knew.~~

—

Doc carries on about triggers

How they *illuminate* the senses

How music makes unsuspecting time travelers out of us

Doesn't it?

Section III: Parenthood

Strange

Is it strange
That I confused
A lit cigarette with refuge?
Swirls of smoke like witch fingers invite me
Into pointless conversations
A yellow film hugs my skin
Like a lemon rind
My hair lined with corks and butts
Family meals don't quite outshine
The charm of a tipped nightcap
At the dinner table
I am eight years old
I am alone
Again at the mall
Shivering in my denim jacket
A creepy man with a wonky gait
Nudges me hard
My folks can't drive after dark
Hoppy fizz is
The culprit of cloudy night vision
I am twelve years old
I am alone
Again at a school play
Guised in renaissance garb
A costume my grandmother sewed
The pupils all went home
I cried into my puffy hat
w a i t i n g
w a i t i n g
w a i t i n g
Faces crinkled with condolence
A palpable pity
I am fourteen years old
I am alone
Is it odd that I mistook boozy babble for belonging?
I am twenty-nine years old
I am not alone
~~In my forgiveness~~

~~Soft feelings~~
My little fawn
I won't be late

Mr. P

Your mother saved your first grade spelling tests circa 1992
The pages are faded & soft yellow like a healing bruise
The childlike penmanship is tender and breaks my heart
~~though I'm not sure why~~
You're not fond of treasure troves
The practice is effusive and that of a hoarder
You prefer to romanticize the future
As if one's history is inanimate
As if the past is merely a plastic appendage
to be plucked from the terracotta head
of Mister Potato
I'd like to believe the past, present and future
are mutually exclusive, too.
But we know better.

Night Is a Woman

Night is a woman
She looks through me
With the inertia of a glass eye
Her illusion of engagement
Is an empty golden iris
I shake her hard
Like a magic eight ball
Waiting for an answer to appear
Just tell me what to do
...tell me what to do
Advice is funny like that
it's
t h e r e
& then
it's
g o n e
gently used
u n w a n t e d
maybe if I take enough
I'll forget the question
She teaches me
To flick away
tiny granules of salty opinions
So I can hear myself think
She's a ruthless bitch
but she's faithful

The Euphemism

I drove myself to the bookstore
& meandered in solitude
zigzagging through the corn maze of book covers
gleaming like polychromatic tiles

—

In the farthest back corner
displayed upon the bottommost shelf
appeared a modest category entitled:
Special Needs
I found it puzzling how
this multidimensional culture/identity/community/topic
is reduced to a crescent thumbnail
& guised as a pillowy euphemism
while simultaneously occupying such vast space
in my life
& the world

—

I kept thinking
This seemingly meager section
Is bursting rich &
Could devour the whole damn building

P.E.

As your kids play succinctly
Following nuanced instructions like so
Mine is sidelined in the sand
Making cakes out of dampened dirt
90's Sheryl said:
If it makes you happy
It can't be that bad
If it makes her happy
Then why the hell am I so sad?
Do not assume playground bakers
Cannot participate with your kids, too
So what if the rules are broken?
~
I wanted to write a poem about inclusion
But ableism is outdated wallpaper affixed to the world
It's impossible to scrape off entirely
But I am tireless
Bubbling up like a hot spring

Frozen

If my shame & sorrow could be contained
in a frozen lake on a dark night
maybe *then*, I could explain:
This—is the landscape of my loneliness
Onlookers see me from afar
a stiff insect encased in a cube of ice
I cannot twirl in frozen darkness
I'm at the mercy of the blonde sun
waiting for mother nature to offer her warmth
and turn over a new day
Feral episodes lasting minutes
are archived deep within my bones
I cry icicle tears
Where does it all go?
As heavy moments
suspend from my interior
I wonder what will become of me
and the snowcapped mountain
I made but cannot carry ~~alone~~

Birdling

How many gratitude-lists
must I write
before my wishes cool
and find dormancy
in the well
from whence they came?
Sometimes wishes fall
as buckling cakes do
And still, a mother heart
kneads her birdling's
clipped wings
peacefully

Feverish

As her mother
I cannot rest until she rests
I cannot function until her fever breaks
Lukewarm bath at midnight
Tiny scoops of Tylenol flavored ice cream
Wait...wait...wait for a sweaty hairline
Visceral wails jolt my nervous system
Even though she is my 2nd
    [I thought I would be stronger]
Milk flowing from my body pacifies
I nurse my need for peace
I nurse my own angst
I nurse a semblance of control
To be plain: I haven't slept in years
I did not know my mother was likely sleep deprived
when I asked so much of her

In my fever dream
I take a whiskey neat
& make eyes at Tony Soprano
Wakeup call at 5:30am
The creamsicle sunrise is unforgiving
She doesn't care if you're a mother
But I do.

Unrest

Everywhere I go
I hear a baby crying
I check to see if it's mine
Even against the backdrop
of a lonesome day
the pulse of humanity
awakens a maternal vigilante
asleep inside my ear
The looming sense of angst
is omnipresent
Does a carer ever rest?
I use white noise
to tamp the primal urge
to scale the walls of my skin
until a swaddle soothes
because the baby
is my anxiety
and without it
I don't know
who's hair
to untangle

Devon Sawa

Night swimming in a bathtub
brimming with regret
No one knows this ceramic tomb
cradles me at 3am
When the air is still
and the only chatter to be heard
are house noises mumbling

Submerged in water
my mind churns like butter
and all of the to's
that I forgot to do
introduce themselves to me:

"Hello Dear,

I am the lunch you forgot to pack, you horse's ass!"

I shoo the failed do's away like shameless flies
They buzz all the way down the drain
along with strands of hair
and unfinished business

Suddenly I'm reminded of
Casper the Friendly Ghost, asking:

"Can I keep you?"

Even ghosts grapple with letting go
A small voice from an ethereal realm says: "stay"
I pay homage to the 90's
as pearls of sweat sprout from my skin
and meld with old bath water

It's been a long night
but I am comforted knowing
that Devon Sawa is still around
and 10 years older than me

Section IV: Spirit & Fortitude

Death to perfection

How is perfection conceived?
I hire an interpreter
To translate its implications
So I can bury it with the worms
Disassembling my expectations
With the precision of a whittler
Carving away dark spots
Sanding down trepidation
Spirals of self-doubt
Coil around the blade
Exposing deepening roots
I wrap my fingers around them
Yanking them all loose
When I gaze upon my dirty palms
I observe its dissolution
Disintegrating into dust
A rapid resolution
Aha!
What we think we know
Is ever-changing
I fluidity that grounds my feet
I cling to this reckoning with a belly breath
A guttural sigh of relief
Exercising a lighthearted skip
The shameless hop of a hare
A sweet and savory process
The thrill of a grade school dare
I untie the rubber band
Which clenches my hair just so
I give it an honest shake
Letting it all fucking go
At last I celebrate my being's function
God damn!
I got gumption

Hot Gun

Looking in the mirror
I held my own gaze
Like a gunslinger anticipating a fast draw
But this isn't a Western &
I refuse to be the understudy
~~of my life~~
Magic hands quicken coz
I am the Cowboy with a hot gun

Beautiful Things

Fragments of mosaic glass
shimmered beneath my bare feet
Sunlit hues of violet embers
grazed my ankles like roadside peonies
I wondered if walking atop broken glass is painful
if it's stained holy
I learned that beautiful things
do the most harm
& took another step

Radio Silence

Radio silence
I take pause
awaiting trivial chatter
to lazily attend
a gap in which choices are made
to stay here [with me] in static
or make out with hapless vices
the in-between keeps her aloft
draped in velvet still
laced with listen…
        listen..
                listen.
this quiet place seems important.

Self-Soothe

I dig trenches along the surface of my brain
Heaving memories like wreckage over my shoulder
Building pathways to new beliefs
I declare undertones of truth
Untangling associations is hairsplitting
Tedious yet necessary to rewrite the narrative I live aloud
I resign to pangs of new growth
Emerging from the follicle
Kinky and strayed unlike the rest
I chant mantras like lyrics of an old show tune
Dancing dizzy to the sound of solace
And when you appear in my periphery
The abandoned paths that were overgrown
Suddenly become worn and well-traveled
Still I sing aloud my becoming
Poking holes in lies I've played out true
Digging out deadened patterns my hands repeat
Still I try coz
Soothing myself is all I can do

Ballerina

Opening my jewelry box
I share secrets with you
Relics of my past sparkling in the light
Fake plastic beads like skittles
Flecks of silver and gold
The ballerina twirls round and round
The same cyclical motion
Devoted to her course
At the mercy of those who don the jewels
Waiting for the lid to crack open
She springs up on cue
The music plays for a while
Tinkering chimes of minor key
Her moment to dance
The darkness is soon upon her
She waits patiently to be freed
What is your name? I ask
But she does not reply
Her porcelain face like a cherub
Perhaps she doesn't mind
For this is all she knows

Anne

Her elbows are pointy like her grandmother's
No matter the skin care regimen
Sugar scrubs, exfoliants, microbeads
The place at which her funny bone intersects the dinner table
Is shadowed, dull and unsightly
For decades her arms are propped up on hard surfaces like a tripod
Balancing her shiny pocked chin
deep in thought...dialogue...study
Or perhaps rounded out like wings with her hands resting
In the divots of her hips
Posing for pictures or giving you the business
How unladylike
She is not sheepish about these unambiguously **bold** blemishes
Because her pointy elbows and pointed wit
Belong to Anne.

Highways

The space between pen and paper
Is where I discover *her*
Flickers of memory reflect onto thin lines of blue
Recollections that live and b r e a t h e
Shadows only seen in perfect lighting
Pay attention
A poet's mind
And photographer's eye
Behold a sacred process
Utterly exposed. submerged
Patiently developing
Birthing the onus of self-awareness
Ownership
She stares into the prose waiting for her image to materialize
She smiles at her familiar face
Burgeoning new lines of truth like highways leading her home

www.ingramcontent.com/pod-product-compliance
Lightning Source LLC
LaVergne TN
LVHW052357100826
845147LV00013B/867
* 9 7 9 8 8 9 9 9 0 5 1 3 1 *